Disney
WHERE'S MY WATER

Swampy's Official
Guide to the Sewers

BANTAM
BOOKS

This handbook
belongs to
the squeaky-clean

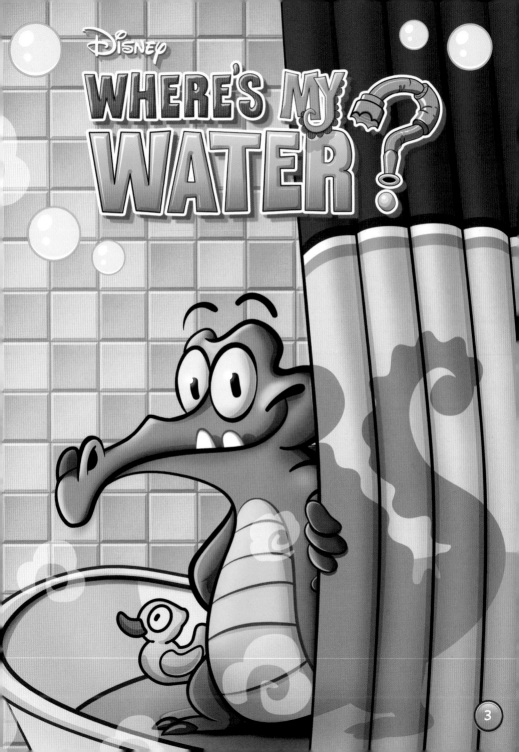

Contents

Welcome to the sewer!

Get ready to play!

Top secret!

Puzzles!

More sew-per fun!

Where's My Water? 2

Taking clean to a new level

Meet Swampy!

All you need to know about our favourite sewer-dweller.

Swampy's style: Swampy is lovable, kind-hearted and above all, he loves to be clean!

Favourite pastime? Waiting for his beloved water to come shooting down and give him a nice bath.

He lives... in a janitors' closet. Close to all those lovely cleaning products.

Did you know?

He's always nice and friendly to the other alligators in the sewer, even when they aren't that nice back!

Prized possession? His bathtub and Ducky.

Meet Allie!

The sweetest alligator this side of the sewer!

She lives...
in the sewers with the rest of the alligators, but she likes to go and visit Swampy now and then.

Allie's style:
Being an alligator doesn't mean you can't accessorise! Chokers are sooo chic!

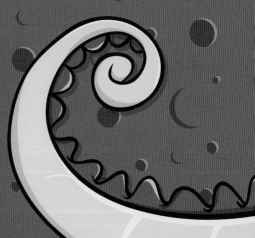

Prized possession?
Her pipe organ —
Allie loves to play music on it!

Did you know?
Allie's full name is Allie Gator... get it?!

Meet Cranky!

Watch out — you're about to learn all about the sewers' hungriest creature!

Favourite pastime? Eating anything he can get his claws on.

Did you know?
Whenever Swampy's water gets stuck, it's usually down to Cranky and his gang.

He lives... In a dark and stinky corner of the sewers.

Cranky's style: Smelly, dirty and mucky. Well, he does live in a sewer!

Prized possession? Ooze. As much of it as he can find!

Did you know?
No one knows how Cranky got the mysterious scar on his tummy... and they're all afraid to ask!

11

Meet Ducky!

Swampy's sidekick and bath time buddy!

Prized possession?
His numerous outfits.
A duck's got to
look good...

Ducky's style:
Ducky is always dressed
for the occasion...
although no one really
knows how — not
even Swampy.

Did you know?

His alter ego is
called Mystery Duck
— a clever magician
who can create a
whole host of
other ducks!

He lives... in Swampy's
bathtub, although
sometimes he does get
stuck in the pipes.

Favourite pastime?
Sloshing around in water.
It's a duck's life.

Did you know?

He's related to
Cranky's Duck
– a purple duck
that hates
water.

SWAMPY'S STORY

Your mission, should you choose to dig it, is to clear a path through the dirt so Swampy can take a nice, hot shower.

Water

Duckies

Broken pipe

To do this, drag your finger from the water (the blue stuff) through the dirt towards the broken pipe.

Simple!

Don't forget to collect the three Duckies along the way by filling them up with water. You'll need five drops of water for each Ducky. Collect all three and you'll tri-duck the level.

Remember: On Swampy's levels, only get water into the pipe — otherwise you end up with one unhappy gator!

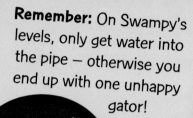

It's different for Allie and Cranky levels though . . . turn to pages 96 and 104 to find out why.

You only need 20 drops of water to go into Swampy's pipe to complete the level. Keep this in mind during the later, more complicated levels. Any extra water goes towards your 'Overflow Bonus'.

There will be obstacles and challenges as you progress through the levels, but never fear — you'll get better with practice! And with over 200 levels to complete, there's lots of opportunity to perfect those digging skills.

On some levels, look out for an extra icon appearing next to the replay button. Press this to play the level as a Mystery Duck level.

Can you dig it?

There's so much more to digging than simply dragging your finger down the screen. Here's a list of need-to-know digging tips.

You can make the water flow at different speeds by cutting different-sized tunnels through the dirt. The wider the tunnel, the faster the water will flow. This is a great technique for getting as much water as possible to another part of the puzzle as quickly as possible.

Remember: How you dig in the dirt will affect how the water flows, so it's worth taking your time and thinking it through!

If you need to direct your water to a specific place for a precision strike or limit the amount of water to somewhere, then it's best to dig as narrow a tunnel as possible. This will make the water flow more slowly.

Sometimes you'll need to save a small amount of water in a certain place in the puzzle for another time — perhaps waiting to get a Ducky until an obstacle clears or waiting to activate a switch at the right time. In this case, dig a little bowl in the dirt to store your water, so it's ready to use when you need it.

Ooze alert! Green ooze burns through dirt but if you clear a path, you can guide it to where you want it to go, avoiding ducks or water pipes.

To learn more about ooze turn to page 20.

Soil, toil and rubble!

Get your feet on solid ground with this guide to playing surfaces.

Dirt

Dirt is water's best friend. You can draw your finger through any mass of dirt and guide the water safely to Swampy. It doesn't affect the water at all and keeps poison water at bay. Watch out for ooze, as this dissolves dirt in a flash!

Rock

Rock can guide water safely to Swampy's pipe. Be careful — explosions will destroy rock and alter the flow of water. You can't cut through it with your finger... Or can you?

Algae

Be careful with this strange plant as it acts differently depending on what flows past it. Water will make it grow bigger, poison water will destroy it, toxic ooze will turn the algae to rock!

Did you know?

When toxic ooze touches algae it forms rock!

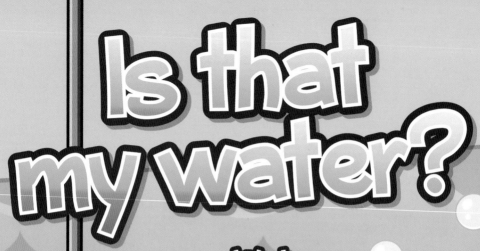

Is that my water?

Water

Water is the only thing that matters in this game. Your aim is to guide it safely to Swampy through his broken pipes. Watch out, it will get contaminated if it touches poison water!

Toxic ooze

Once you reach Troubled Waters you will come into contact with toxic ooze. No one knows what this mysterious substance is, but it has lots of uses! Mixed with poison water, it will make an explosion. Mixed with algae, it will create rock. But get it anywhere near Swampy's pipe and it's game over!

Not all liquids in the sewer will give Swampy the baths he loves — some can be downright dangerous!

Poison water

Poison water can be useful — guide it through the level to clear algae out of the way or mix it with toxic ooze to create explosions. But beware of getting it too near to Swampy's pipe or you'll lose the level!

Mud

Mud is dirt that has become so wet it can move around like water. It jets out of pipes and hardens into dirt if it's left alone for a while. You won't have to deal with mud until later in the game, so you've got lots of time to practise before handling this tricky substance!

Did you know?

Poison water will destroy Ducky!

Watch out!

Mines!

Buried deep within the sewer system lie these un-exploded mines, just waiting to cause mayhem with your game. They are activated when any type of fluid hits them, so try and use them to your advantage to get rid of unwanted items or rock. Be careful around Ducky, as mines will destroy him!

Thorns!

Although thorns don't grow like algae, they can't be destroyed by poison water either! You can use these tricky plants to pop balloons as you get further into the game.

As if Cranky and his band of alligators wasn't enough, there are also lots of hazards stopping Swampy from getting a nice hot bath. Read up and take note!

Wheels

Shooting liquid from these colour-coded wheels can either help or harm your water-grabbing attempts. You need to work out what each wheel contains before you can really use it to your advantage.

Collectibles!

It's amazing what gets washed up in the sewers and Swampy loves to collect unusual things. As soon as you see something interesting as you're digging, uncover it completely to find out what it is. You'll need to successfully complete the level before it will go into your collection.

Collection   Bonus Levels

1

"Meet Swampy"

2

"Meet Swampy"

3

"Troubled Waters"

Want to know which level each collectible is hidden in? Look no further than the next three pages.

Collectible name • Level number • Level name

 Shiny Scale Shampoo • 1-7 • Drain It First

 Suds-a-Lot Soap • 1-10 • Split Decision

 Lucky Loofah • 1-12 • Divide & Conquer

 Toothbrush • 1-14 • Loop the Loop

 Minty Icing • 1-16 • Three Scoops

 Finicky Floss • 1-19 • Seesaw

 Lazy Flipper • 2-4 • Long Journey

 Nessie • 2-8 • One Stream

 Reading Goggles • 2-10 • Make a Wave

 Party Hat • 2-14 • Mind the Gap

 Life Preserver • 2-15 • Boomerang

Scope • 2-20 • Half and Half

Picnic Basket • 3-3 • Ooze Fall

Talk Box • 3-5 • Bomb Chain

Sugary Soap • 3-8 • Let's Play Catch

Spoon-apault • 3-12 • Bomb It Up!

Chip • 3-15 • Going Down?

Momma Teapot • 3-18 • Untimely Growth

 Bow • 4-1 • Logic Gates

Back Scratcher • 4-4 • Bridge Builder

Look out for the question mark alongside the Duckies when you're playing the level. That means there's a collectible to find!

Poetry Perfume • 4-9 • Curse of the Algae Beard

Heart-shaped Box • 4-15 • Figure Eight

 Rose • 4-17 • The Grid

Teddy Bear • 4-20 • Rinse Cycle

Big Apple • 5-2 • Recycling Works

Artistic Woman • 5-5 • Bottleneck

Tiny Taxi • 5-8 • One Way Street

Gyration Junkie • 5-12 • Scaffolding

Multipurpose Hat • 5-14 • Double Dip

Scooter Penrose • 5-17 • Pick Your Poison

The Glider • 6-2 • Steam Cleaning

Claw Cleaners • 6-4 • Rise and Fall

Hypothesis Hat • 6-8 • Through the Bridge

Water Cloth • 6-12 • Revolving Door

Golden Locks • 6-15 • Ventilation Shaft

All Terrain Marker • 6-19 • Through and Through

Time Travelling Hat • 7-4 • Balloon Bridge

Cone of Authority • 7-6 • Down the Hatch

Plot Device • 7-10 • Mirror Image

One Man Band • 7-14 • Pipe Organ

Good Morning Machine • 7-16 • Be Careful Burning Bridges

 Heartbreak Accelerator • 7-20 • Balloon Gauntlet

 Polka Dot Stamp • 8-3 • Updraft

 Soup Bowl • 8-5 • On and Off

 Hand Flipper • 8-8 • Wind Power

 Rotisserie Rotators • 8-11 • Freefallin'

 Figurine Head • 8-14 • Ice Pit

 Pandora's Box • 8-17 • Headwind

 Lazy Music Box • 9-2 • Mix it UP!

 Magnet Carrying Case • 9-4 • One Shot Wonder

 Bread Launcher • 9-9 • Stop and Drop

 Domino the Fragile Dog • 9-11 • Rainmaker

 Party Horn • 9-16 • Steam Splitter

 Day of Cake Hat • 9-20 • Full of Hot Air

 Squishy Fishy • 10-3 • Cut and Dry

 Snout Guard • 10-6 • Muddy Journey

 Tail Floatation Device • 10-8 • Can You Dig It?

 Double-scope • 10-12 • Make a Ramp

 Twisted Time Teller! • 10-14 • Misty Mud

 Portable Campfire • 10-17 • Landfill

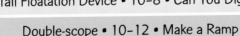

Go to Swampy's collectible shelf. If you've found all three collectibles on a shelf, you unlock a bonus level, for more water-based fun!

Top 10 squeaky clean tips!

The 10 things every WMW gamer needs to know!

1 Time is water!

As the levels get trickier, you may want to take some time to work out what to do before the game starts, especially if you have ooze eating its way towards Swampy's pipe! Don't be afraid to hit the 'pause' button and take a good look at what needs to be done!

2 Where is my collection?

It's super exciting when you discover a collectible, but watch out — if you're not careful your newly uncovered booty will disappear as soon as it is found! If you don't manage to complete the level, your collectible will go right back into the dirt.

3 Try, try and try again!

Do you know one of the best things about WMW? No matter how many times you leave Swampy bone dry, or get more water on Cranky's plate or clog up Allie's organ pipes with ooze, they'll always be ready to go again. So, if at first you don't succeed, try, try again!

4 Swot up

It's really tempting to start rushing through levels when you think you've got the hang of the game, but that's when things can start to go wrong... Suddenly, there's a whole new element you haven't seen before! Why not read through this guide to get ready for whatever Cranky and his gang can throw at you?

Duck the ducks

Tri-ducking is great and can unlock loads of extra levels and features, but it can be tricky to get all the ducks, first time round. If you're finding it really hard, why not complete the level and go onto the next? You might find that the better you become at the game, the easier it will be to go back and get all the ducks next time round!

6 Controlled explosion

When they first appear, you might want to avoid the mines and their explosive reactions. However, the further you get, you'll realise that they can be used to your advantage! It may take a few tries, but hitting a mine just right might be the only way to complete a level!

7 Mechanical magic

These strange looking objects have a lot of different functions, which might not immediately be apparent. Drop water into the funnel mechanism to make it start, and push water against the buttons of the push mechanism to see what happens. The blue and white mechanism moves when you drag your finger across it.

Change pipe

You'll find this pipe as you reach the half-way stage of the game, and it's a real head-scratcher! Regardless of what you fire into the pipe, it will change into whatever is pictured on the pipe's mechanism. Sometimes these pipes come with a button, which lets you change what comes out the other end.

⑨ Balloons

Balloons are a complex item to use in gameplay and have a lot of different functions. They can be filled with water, poison water or steam. When filled with water the balloon remains red, if it's got poison water inside a little skull will appear, and when it's full of steam it will display a cloud. Watch out — when filled with steam the balloon will float up instead of down! Balloons can be popped when they hit ice or hot coals (see below), thorns, or are squished between mechanisms.

⑩ Fire and ice

The hot coals are used to make any liquid turn into steam. The ice turns steam into water, no matter what liquid was used to create the steam. Unlike water, steam will get stuck if it hits dirt or rock, so make sure it has a clean path. When it transforms back into water it will fall downwards, so it's best to draw your path before making steam!

Lost levels!

The following pages reveal the secret entrances to some amazing hidden levels!

Planetarium

To reach a level that's out of this world, click the 'achievements' button when scrolling through the levels. Scroll your thumb down to reveal a planet symbol hidden at the top of the page. Click on this to reveal the Planetarium level.

Missing Laser

This level can be found in Cranky's story, at the top of the challenges screen. Scroll up until you see a skull symbol. Click on the skull to discover the hidden level.

Ups and Downs

When reviewing your collection, scroll to the top of the page to reveal a pair of arrows — one going up and one going down. Click on the arrows to reveal an explosive level!

Sara's Level

To reveal Sara's secret level, you will need to be in Cranky's story. When you are on the food groups page, scroll to the top and click on the flower symbol. Get ready for a fiery ride!

Every Which Way

To unlock this level you'll need to be in the free version of the game. Go to your collectibles and scroll down until you see a shape carved into the wood. Click on that to discover more fun!

Mysterious Planets

When you click into the Mystery Duck version of the game, you will see a doodle of a planet with a top hat. Click on this to complete the Planetarium level with a mega Ducky!

Good Morning & Underground Adventure

In the collectibles menu, scroll all the way down to the bottom of the shelves. First you will see a sunshine doodle carved into the wood – this is the entrance to the secret Good Morning level! Scroll down even further to reveal a fire extinguisher; this will take you to the Underground Adventure level.

Did you know?
Each time you update WMW there could be new levels to find!

Turn to page 102 for more lost levels.

TOP SECRET

Achievements!

There are lots of extra items to discover while you play. Check out these secret achievements!

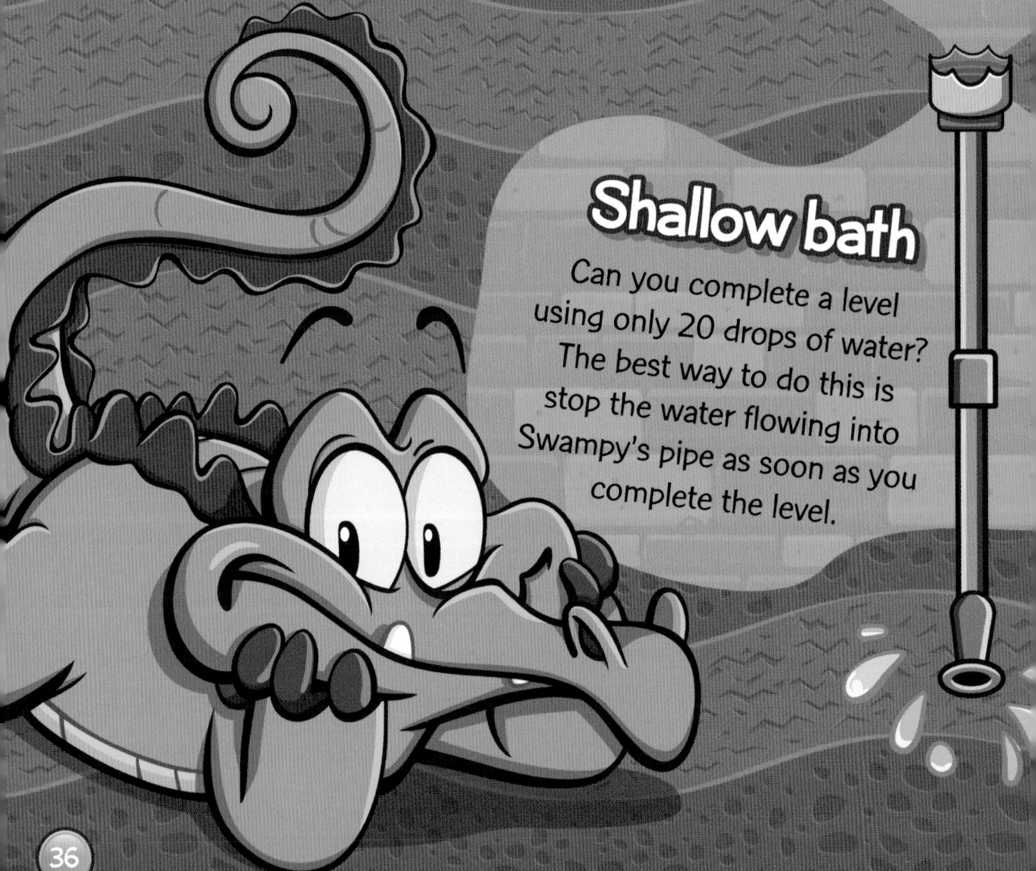

Shallow bath

Can you complete a level using only 20 drops of water? The best way to do this is stop the water flowing into Swampy's pipe as soon as you complete the level.

Poison water

To get this achievement takes time. You need to drop poison water into Swampy's bath tub 20 times!

Embarrassed

Make Swampy hide behind his shower curtain! All you need to do is to tap Swampy repeatedly once water has started to flow into his pipe.

Confidence

Complete level 2-7 (What Goes Up) without taking your finger off the screen... this might take a bit of practice!

Quick finish

Go to level 3-17 (Back and Forth) and complete it in 20 seconds or less.

Efficient cut

Just cut through the dirt with two fingers at a time. Simple!

Good to the last drop

Complete level 2-9 (One Step at a Time) without losing a single drop of water!

OCD

Try, and fail, a level seven times before getting it on the last go. Use an easy level to gain this achievement.

Who made this?

So easy you could do it with your eyes closed! Sort of. Go to the Settings menu and watch the credits. That's all!

Easter Eggs

There's lots of fun to be had when you're not moving water around a sewer! Check out these secret extras!

Hello Swampy!

Get to know our hero better. When you are in the Swampy's Story menu, all you have to do is tap on Swampy to make him do something different. Sometimes he'll laugh, or shiver, but watch out — if you bother him too much he might get angry!

Cranky's chuckles

On levels where you need to scroll up and down, you can discover a cheeky chuckling Cranky! Scroll to the bottom of the level, then keep scrolling down. Cranky can be seen hiding under Swampy!

Quack, quack, quack!

Radio

Most of the time, the radio will send out quacking sounds when you tap it, but if you have the free version of the game, and you play at Christmas, you will hear the ducks quacking out some very tuneful Christmas carols!

Don't cry, Swampy!

If you fail a level, Swampy tends to get a little upset! Watch out to see how he reacts. Sometimes, if he's really in need of a bath, he'll let out a really big wail!

Cranky's spotlight

When you complete a level in Cranky's story, a spotlight will appear creating Cranky's silhouette. You can move this around with your finger!

Tri-duck

If you're skilful enough to tri-duck (get all three ducks) in a chapter, a special duck symbol will appear on the home screen. If you tap it, the duck will laugh and quack!

Shower power

If you tap Swampy's shower head on the home screen, little droplets of water will come out.

Swampy's graffiti

Swampy has been etching his name on some of his furniture. Scroll to the very bottom of the collectibles shelves to discover his mark!

Broken pipes!

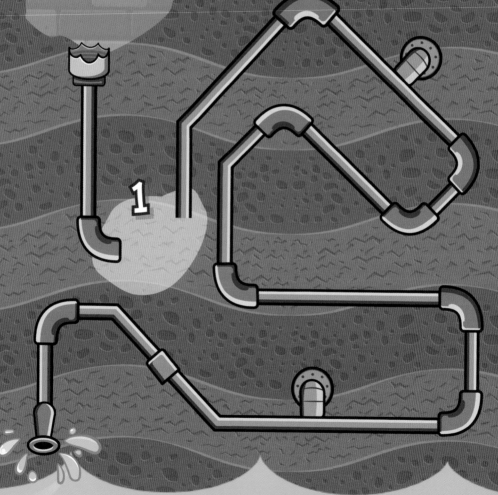

If you want to carry on gaming, please turn to page 96.

It's time to help Swampy get clean! Take a look at the tangle of pipes and work out which pieces are needed to help the water flow smoothly.

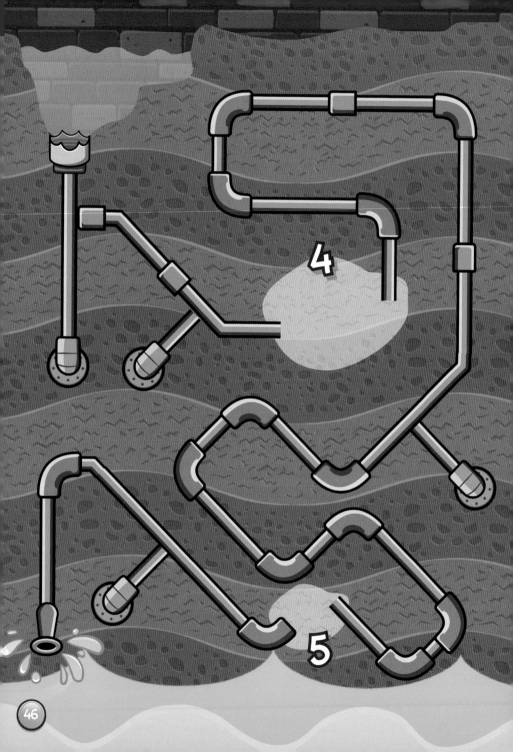

Answers on page 94

Swampy's experiments!

Cranky's crossed words

Can you fit all of the words into the grid? We've done the first one for you!

Biting
Cranky
Smelly
Dirty
Trash
Rotten
Sabotage
Sewer

b
i
t
i
n
g

Did you know?
Counting the letters in each word will help you solve the puzzle!

Mystery Duck's magic tricks!

Want to be as mysterious as Mystery Duck? See if you can impress your friends with these simple tricks!

Card crumple

Take a pack of cards and ask a friend to pick one out and look at it, but make sure that you don't see it. When they hand the card back to you, secretly bend the card slightly. Shuffle the pack of cards, then look through it as though you are searching for your friend's card. When you come to the bent card, pull it out!

Paper friends

You'll need to perform this trick with a partner, but don't let your other friends know you are in on it together. Ask your friends to stand in a circle and put a piece of paper in the middle. Now leave the room and ask one of your friends to secretly pick up the paper and put it in their pocket. Come back in and slowly walk around the circle as though you are trying to work out who the 'Paper Friend' is. Your partner must scratch his nose when you are behind the right friend and... ta-da! Everyone will think you can see through walls!

Mind reader!

Convince your friends you can read their minds by asking them the following questions:

- Think of a number between **1** and **10**
- Multiply it by **2**
- Add **10**
- Divide it by **2**
- Now, take away the first number you thought of
- Now say **"The number you are left with is 5!"**

See how surprised your friends will be!

Word ladder

SWAMPY
S_A_P_
ST_ _ _S
S_ _MP_
SLUMPS

CLUMPS
C_A_ _S
C_A_ _ _
C_ _ _PS
CRI_ _S

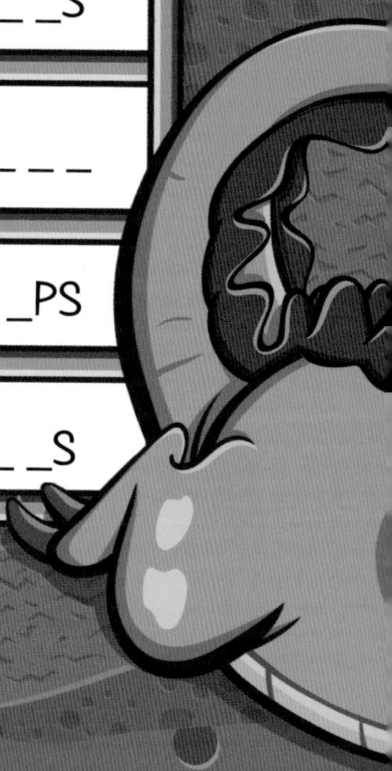

Can you complete these word ladders to get from 'Swampy' to 'Cranky' by changing only one letter at a time?

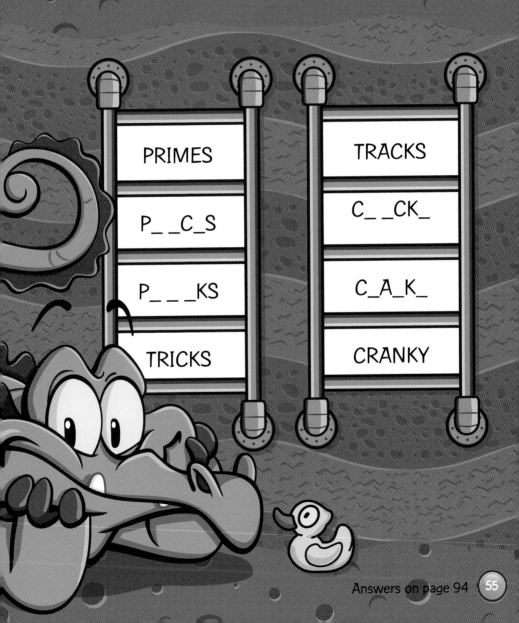

PRIMES

P _ _ C _ S

P _ _ _ KS

TRICKS

TRACKS

C _ _ CK _

C _ A _ K _

CRANKY

Answers on page 94

Cranky's crew

a

b

c

d

Cranky's been taking bites out of
this picture! Can you work out
which pieces go where?

Answers on page 94

Gurgling giggles!

Swampy and Ducky will quack you up
with these funny jokes!

Q: Why do robots hate
having baths?
A: They get rusty nails!

Q: Who gives
alligators presents
at Christmas?
A: Santa Jaws!

Q: Which villains steal
soap from the bath?
A: Robber ducks!

Q: What do ducks say
at the end of a meal?
A: Put it on my bill!

Troubled waters

Uh oh, Swampy's desperate to get back to his janitors' closet, but he wants to stay as clean as possible!

9

8
Short cut! Shimmy along the pipe and move to space 12!

1
Start

2

3
Great start, you've found some soap! Move forward two spaces.

- Place buttons or small coins on the start square.
- The youngest player goes first.
- Roll a dice and move around the board, following the instructions on each square you land on.
- The first player to get to the janitors' closet is the winner!

10
You've spotted an extra-nice bow for Allie — go back three spaces to get it.

11

12

13
Almost at the closet. Slither forward one to get there sooner!

7

6
Ewww, you've slipped in something slimy. Stay put for one go to wipe it off.

14

15
You win!

5

4

Water way to go!

What's wrong?

Take a look at these pictures of Cranky, Allie and Swampy and see if you can spot the one thing that is wrong in each pic!

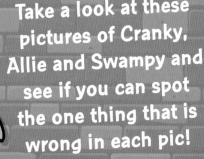

Answers on page 94

Number square

Each row, column and diagonal must total 15. Can you work out the missing squares?

Answers on page 94

Swampy's Search

Swampy

Pipes

Algae

Allie

Sewer

Cranky

Ducky

Ooze

Dirt   Water

S	D	C	V	H	J	E	Z	O	O
S	E	W	E	R	K	U	T	G	S
C	V	N	Y	K	C	U	D	B	W
C	D	O	A	L	G	A	E	N	A
R	G	J	O	L	S	E	P	H	M
A	H	I	N	E	L	G	B	T	P
N	B	D	V	B	N	I	M	H	Y
K	N	Q	I	W	R	E	E	T	B
Y	F	E	S	R	E	T	A	W	M
P	I	P	E	S	T	A	E	L	E

Feelin' Cranky!

Only two of these Crankys
are exactly the same.
Can you spot them?

a

b

c

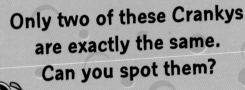

Did you know?

Cranky loves
nothing more than
chomping his way
through the left-over
food he finds in the
swamp! Yuk!

Draw Swampy!

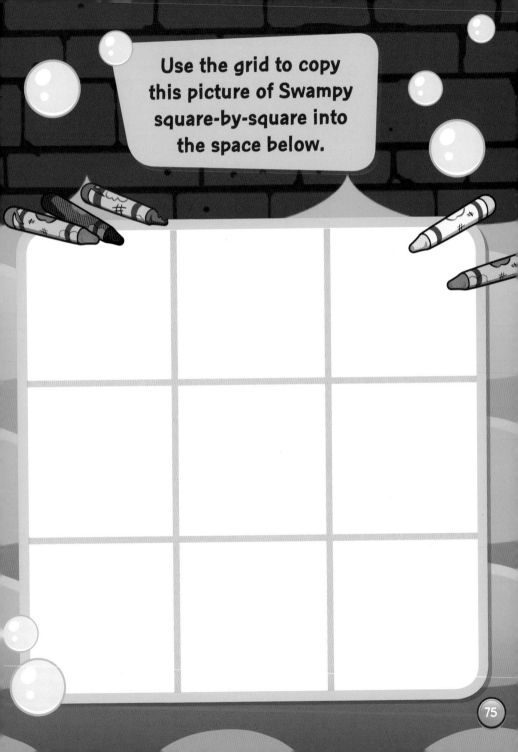

Use the grid to copy this picture of Swampy square-by-square into the space below.

Lunch time!

Basket ☐   Tin ☐   Starfish ☐

Take a close look at this picture and see
if you can spot all the things in the list.
Tick them off as you go!

Answers on page 94

Drain ☐ Candle ☐ Fish ☐

Design your own level!

Time to get inventive! Design your own level using the space opposite. How hard can you make it?

Ducky?

Don't forget to add three little Duckies to your level!

Dirt or rock?

Use brown pencils or crayons for the dirt sections, and purple for the rock. Remember you can only drag through dirt!

Once you have perfected your level, pass it on to a friend to see if they can solve it.

Difficulty?

What obstacles will you put in the way of Swampy getting his water? Mines? Ooze? Algae? The choice is yours!

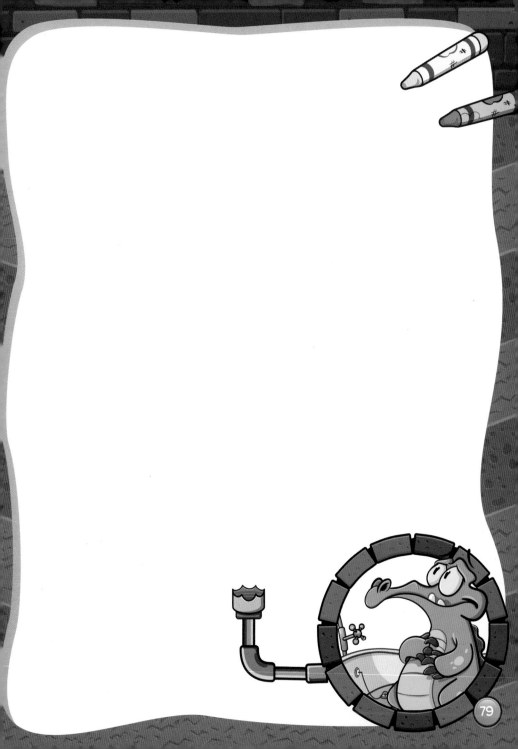

Hearts and crafts

Swampy is busy making a Valentine's card! Can you find six differences between these two pictures?

How clean

Starting at the toothbrush, follow the flow to work out just how clean you really are!

Ever wear the same clothes twice?

Yes

Love splashing about in the bath?

Yes

No

Yes

Brush your teeth twice a day?

Ever leave smelly socks hanging around?

No

Yes

No

Yes

Shampoo?

No

Do you always do the washing up?

are you?

No

Yes →

Swampy

Just like Swampy, you love to be squeaky clean! Just remember it's fun to get messy now and then.

Your room is always spotless!

No →

Allie

Like Allie, you know it's important to be clean, but it doesn't stop you enjoying yourself.

Yes

No →

Ducks are for wimps!

Cranky

What's that smell? It doesn't matter, you're used to it! Being clean is boring in your book! Make sure you brush your teeth now and then or they might fall out.

Yes

No

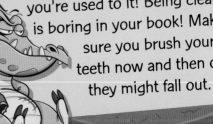

83

Lost property

Can you work out what has been
lost in the sewer? Match the
mixed-up word to the picture.

APLEP

RTUPEMT

LISTCPIK

LCOEV

OTCHR

AHT

Allie's teapot!

Allie's lost her favourite teapot. Read the clues to work out which one is hers!

a

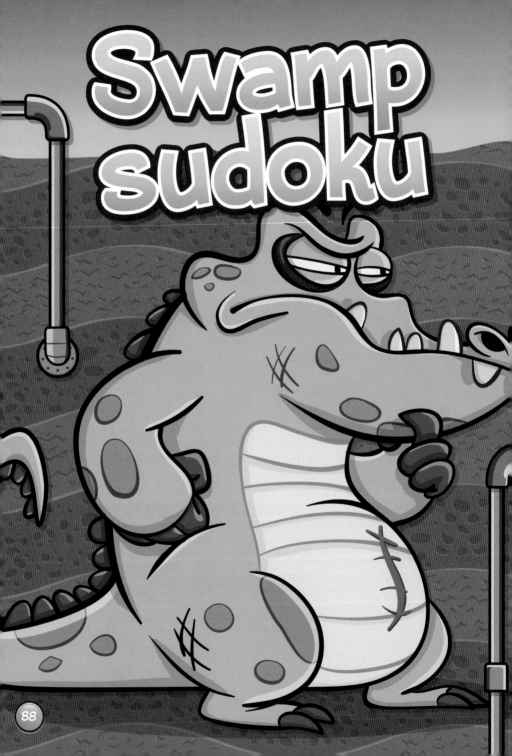

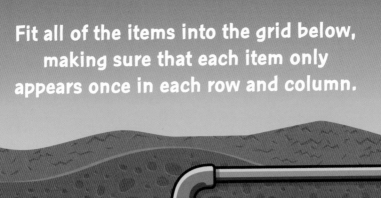

Fit all of the items into the grid below,
making sure that each item only
appears once in each row and column.

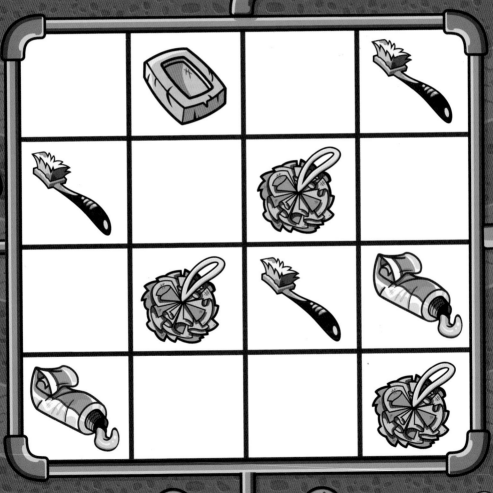

Ducks' delight

Ducky has invited some friends over for a swim! How many can you count?

Answers on page 94

Where's my quiz?

1 Where does Swampy live?

2 What's Allie's prized possession?

3 How does Cranky like to break Swampy's pipes?

4 What's the only way to get through rock?

5 What happens when ooze or poison water gets into Swampy's bath?

6 How do you get to the Planetarium level?

7 What does Swampy love in his bath?

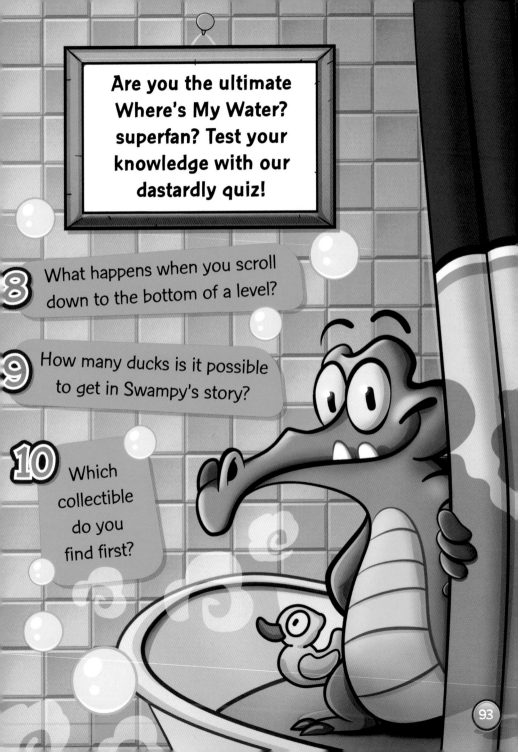

Are you the ultimate Where's My Water? superfan? Test your knowledge with our dastardly quiz!

8 What happens when you scroll down to the bottom of a level?

9 How many ducks is it possible to get in Swampy's story?

10 Which collectible do you find first?

Answers

27 Collectibles
The items are hidden on pages:
9, 12, 23, 37, 52, 63, 81, 87

44-47 Broken pipes
1b, 2c, 3a
4b, 5a, 6d, 7c

48-49 Swampy's experiment

50-51 Crossed words

```
                c       s
                r       m
    s     s a b o t a g e
e               n       l
w     d i r t y k       l
e               i       y
r o t t e n     g
        r
        a
        s
        h
```

54-55 Word ladder

SWAMPY	CLUMPS
SWAMPS	CLAMPS
STAMPS	CRAMPS
STUMPS	CRIMPS
SLUMPS	CRIMES

54-55 Word ladder (continued)

PRIMES	TRACKS
PRICES	CRACKS
PRICKS	CRANKS
TRICKS	CRANKY

56-57 Cranky's crew

62-63 Water way to go!

64-65 What's wrong?

68-69 Number square

8	1	6
3	5	7
4	9	2

70-71 Swampy's search

S	D	C	V	H	J	E	Z	O	O
S	E	W	E	R	K	U	T	G	S
C	V	N	Y	K	C	U	D	B	W
C	D	O	A	L	G	A	E	N	A
R	G	J	O	L	S	E	P	H	M
A	H	I	N	E	L	G	B	T	P
N	B	D	V	B	N	I	M	H	Y
K	N	Q	I	W	R	E	E	T	B
Y	F	E	S	R	E	T	A	W	M
P	I	P	E	S	T	A	E	L	E

72-73 Feelin' Cranky
'a' and 'g' are the same

76-77 Lunch time!

80-81 Hearts and crafts

84-85 Lost property
Apple, Trumpet, Lipstick, Glove, Torch, Hat.

86-87 Allie's teapot
Teapot 'd' is Allie's teapot

88-89 Swamp sudoku

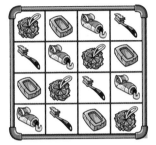

90-91 Ducks' delight
There are 30 ducks.

92-93 Where's my quiz?
1. In the janitors' closet.
2. Her pipe organ.
3. By chewing through them!
4. Blast it!
5. You lose the level
6. It's hidden at the bottom of the achievements screen
7. Water, bubbles and Ducky
8. You find a giggling Cranky
9. 660
10. Lucky Loofah

ALLIE'S STORY

There are lots of similarities with Swampy's levels, so don't worry! You still have to cut through the dirt to guide the substance to the broken pipe and your aim is still to tri-duck every level.

But, there is a twist . . . Allie needs steam to power her pipe organ. So your mission is to cut through the dirt and direct the steam up towards the broken pipe. Maybe you'll have already played a level with steam in *Swampy*'s or *Cranky's Story* – in which case you'll be an expert.

96

You will need 20 droplets of steam to start the organ tootin' and complete the level. When you do, Allie will treat you to a lovely tune!

A 'droplet' is the smallest amount of steam that can be formed.

Allie's Duckies

Fill up these steam-lovin' Duckies with steam to tri-duck the level. Water doesn't hurt Allie's Duckies (it doesn't fill them up either), but poison water and ooze will do. As with Swampy's Duckies, you need five 'droplets' of steam to fill them up.

On some of Allie's levels, a music note button will appear in the top right-hand corner of the game screen. Press this to play this level as an *Allie's Challenge* level — see page 100 for more details.

Music box

During *Allie's Story*, there are lots of musical instruments hidden in the dirt. When you uncover these and complete the level, they'll be added to Allie's 'Music Box'. Collect them all and make Allie's big band dreams come true . . . Here's where to find each one.

Triangle • Level A1-2 • Crossing Streams

Xylophone • Level A1-5 • Down is Up

Tambourine • Level A1-9 • Fan with a Plan

Tuba • Level A1-13 • Crystal Cavern

Drum • A1-15 • BBQ Grill

Cymbals • A1-20 • Wait for It...

Saxophone • A2-1 • Where's My Steam?

Harmonica • A2-4 • Wrapped in a Bow

Piano • A2-7 • Clear the Way

Ukulele • A2-9 • Making the Rounds

Violin • A2-13 • Round the Bend

Harp • A2-20 • Tic Tac Toe

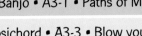

Banjo • A3-1 • Paths of Mine

Harpsichord • A3-3 • Blow your Mine

Trombone • A3-5 • Open and Shut

Xylophone • A3-9 • Fan Boy

 Drum kit • A3-13 • Do Not Touch

Guitar • A3-19 • Time Bomb

Didgeridoo • A4-1 • Switching Sides

Pan Flute • A4-8 • Ready to Rock?

Bagpipes • A4-10 • Race Against Slime

 Maracas • A4-13 • Balloon Over Troubled Borders

Congas • A4-14 • A Coal Out of Reach

Sitar • A4-20 • Smells like Steam Spirit

Did you know?

In 'Music Box', if you've collected all three instruments in a group you'll unlock a bonus level where you have to tilt your device to get the steam around the puzzle.

Allie's challenges

Click on 'Challenges' in *Allie's Story* to discover lots of new challenges and levels!

There are eight different challenges. Each challenge has three levels which you'll already have played either in *Allie's*, *Swampy's* or *Cranky's Story*. But now, get ready to face these again with an additional music twist.

Instead of Duckies, collect five different-coloured music notes in the order shown in the top left of the screen. Just like Duckies, they take five drops to fill up. You'll lose the level if you collect a note out of order!

Depending on whose level you're playing, you can fill up the music notes with water, poison water or steam; water on a Swampy level, poison water on a Cranky level or steam on an Allie level.

When you've completed the challenge levels, you unlock a bonus song. There are two 'free' songs, 'Whistle Whilst in the Shower' and 'Chopsticks', which you'll have heard Allie singing at the end of a level. As you complete the challenges, you can unlock the following songs, which Allie will start to sing when at the end of the level:

CHALLENGE 1 The Bare Necessities

CHALLENGE 2 London Bridge

CHALLENGE 3 Yo Ho (A Pirate's Life for Me)

CHALLENGE 4 Frère Jacques

CHALLENGE 5 Pop Goes the Weasel

CHALLENGE 6 Entertainer

CHALLENGE 7 Beethoven's Fifth

CHALLENGE 8 It's a Small World After All

Lost levels 2

TOP SECRET

You've already read about some of the lost levels . . .
Would you like some more? Of course you would!

Egg and Spoon

A level without an egg or a spoon! If you go to 'Music Box' in *Allie's Story* and scroll right down to the bottom, a little sketch of Allie appears. Tap on this to discover the 'Egg and Spoon' lost level.

One with Everything

A level to match Cranky's huge appetite! Go to 'Food Groups' in *Cranky's Story*, scroll down to the bottom and you'll discover a little sketch of Cranky. Tap on this and get ready for a level which throws everything at you!

Lost Levels

Remember the old 'Level of the Week' feature or the additional festive WMW apps '10 Days of Swampy', 'Hearts and Crafts' and 'Days of Summer'? They were great, weren't they? Well, there's no need to be nostalgic for levels past and lost, because in the paid app you have all of them! Scroll all the way to the right in the game home screen and click on 'Lost Levels' to rediscover the lost tri-duckin' fun!

CRANKY'S STORY

All that time Cranky spent stopping Swampy from having a shower has made him hungry. But the sewers are damp and dirty places so mould has grown over his food. YUCK! Cranky will happily eat anything, from rotten food to stacks of tyres, but mouldy food is a step too far even for him.

Your mission on Cranky's levels is to guide the poison water to his plate so he can enjoy a tasty mould-free meal.

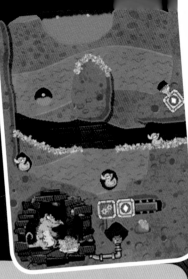

Cranky's Ducky

These Duckies work in the same way as Swampy's Rubber Ducky and Allie's steam Ducky, but they love poison water instead. Water and green ooze will destroy them. Fill them up with five drops of poison water and tri-duck every level!

If any water gets onto Cranky's plate, then the mould will grow, just as it does in the levels. Then you're in danger because Cranky will be hungry AND angry! So, if you don't want to become Cranky's meal instead, then only get poison water in the pipe.

Remember: you only need 20 drops of poison water to complete the level.

If you see a skull button at the top right of the screen (next to the replay button), press it to try the level as a *Cranky Challenge* level.

Food groups

Cranky will eat ANYTHING, even things you uncover in the dirt of the sewers. Here's where to find some tasty morsels in *Cranky's Story*.

Tyre • C1-2 • Meet Me in the Middle

License Plate • C1-4 • Lawn Sprinkler

Muffler • C1-7 • Touch and Hold

Apple Core • C1-12 • Connect the Dots

Banana Peel • C1-15 • The Long Drop

Watermelon Rind • C1-18 • Spillover

Telephone • C2-3 • Recycle

Shoe • C2-5 • Rendezvous

Hairdryer • C2-8 • Spin the Dials

Safe • C2-11 • Volcano

Can • C2-14 • Vicious Cycle

Lunchbox • C2-16 • Worthless Water

Burger • C3-3 • Waterfall

French Fries • C3-6 • Raincatcher

Soda • C3-9 • Gusher

Plunger • C3-11 • Boxed In

Toilet Brush • C3-14 • Unleash the Ooze

Toilet Paper • C3-17 • Cross the Streams

Paper Boat • C4-2 • Don't Be Greedy

Anchor • C4-4 • Acid Rain

Pirate Hat • C4-7 • Water Catcher

Jelly • C4-11 • Wind Shield

Lollipop • C4-14 • Wind Bucket

Birthday Cake • C4-16 • Poison Gauntlet

The more 'Food Groups' you collect, the greater the variety of foods Cranky will eat at the end of the level. It's a good way to make sure he's getting a balanced diet.

Cranky's challenges

Click on 'Challenges' in *Cranky's Story* to discover lots of new challenges and levels!

There are eight different challenges, each with three levels which you'll have already played in either *Allie*'s, *Swampy*'s or *Cranky's Story*. Play these levels with a Cranky twist.

The challenge levels include:

- Tri-duck a Swampy level, with Cranky's ducks.

- Run out of water without getting any to Swampy.

- Complete the level without getting any ducks.

- Complete the level without using switches or balloons.

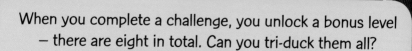

When you complete a challenge, you unlock a bonus level — there are eight in total. Can you tri-duck them all?

DISNEY
WHERE'S MY WATER? 2

You can never have too much of a good thing . . .
so luckily there's a whole new game, full of new
levels, challenges, duckies and gators. Read on
and soon you'll be tri-duckin' every level!

Join the gators as they explore the sewer . . .
and beyond!

New Locations

The exciting new locations include:

The Sewer

The Beach

The Soap Factory

Winter Woods

The Bayou

As you float along the canal by unlocking and completing new levels, your position is marked by your very own Rubber Ducky! Learn about how to choose your Ducky and unlock new outfits on page 124.

Travel between locations through the tunnels at either end of each location. They are helpfully labelled to show where the tunnel takes you!

Levels and Challenges

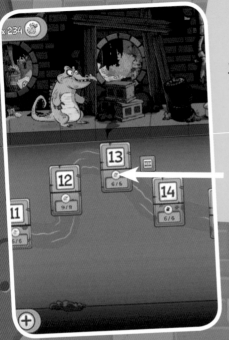

As you click on each level, it opens up a choice of levels. As you complete a level or challenge, it unlocks the next challenge.

If you tri-duck the level and all the challenges, the level in the canal will get a Ducky badge.

Turn to page 116 to learn about the challenges you'll face.

Gates

To unlock the gates between levels and locations, you need to collect a certain number of Duckies. For some gates, for example the gate before you can travel to the Beach, you need keys from your friends. Alternatively, you can buy keys in the store.

Beach

Collectibles

When you find a collectible in the levels, it is displayed proudly on the canal side. Nice! Tap on each collectible to learn more about them.

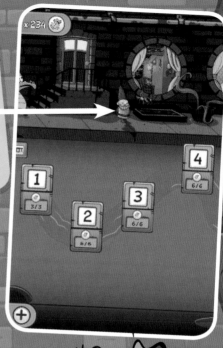

Video Replay

You can replay the videos by pressing on the video button.

The levels

Each level on WMW2 is either a Swampy, a Cranky or an Allie level. You can tell which level is which from the home screen — Swampy levels are blue, Allie's are orange and Cranky's are green. When you complete a level, you unlock a challenge level.

Turn to page 116 to learn all about the challenge levels.

SWAMPY

CRANKY

ALLIE

There are a lot of new, awesome features in WMW2 which add another level of clean! But don't worry, it's not a whole new world, there are some familiar features too.

DUCK RUSH

A new level for WMW2 — It's fast, it's tense, it's a double tri-ducking dash!

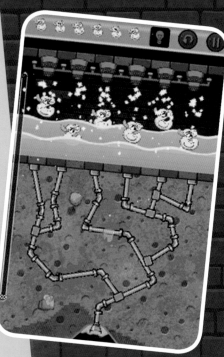

The screen moves down automatically (or up on Allie's 'Duck Rush' levels) and your goal is to keep the water, poison water or steam on screen throughout the level. You only need a few drops to get into the pipe at the end to complete it — this level is all about the ducks! There are six ducks per 'Duck Rush' level — think of it as a double tri-duck level . . . because hex-duck doesn't have quite the same ring to it.

Think fast, avoid obstacles and collect Duckies — this is a level for fast diggers only!

Turn back to page 16 to brush up on your digging skills.

CHALLENGES

When you've successfully completed a level, a new challenge will be unlocked. If you choose to play these, this is what you'll face . . .

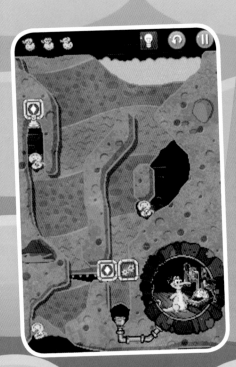

Upside Down!

The level you've just completed gets flipped upside down! Gravity works the opposite way too – so liquids travel upwards and steam travels down! You'll find that the Duckies are in new positions too – so you'll need to turn your wits upside down and inside out to find a new solution to this familiar level.

Driller

You have to complete the level without using any of the switches. All the rock is turned to dirt in these levels, so you can dig anywhere. **Hint:** liquids cannot flow around the pipes, so you'll have to dig a path around them.

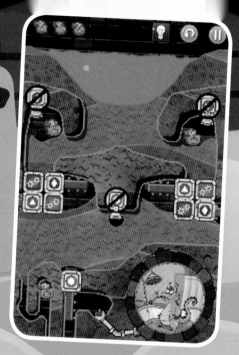

Avoid It!

Complete the level again, but this time avoid all the Duckies. Be careful, one drop on a Ducky and the game is over!

There are no challenges for 'Duck Rush' levels.

Melody

♫ Just like the Challenge levels in *Allie's Story*, you have to collect five different-coloured music notes in order. Like Duckies, they take five drops to fill them up. The order of the notes can be seen in the top left of the screen.

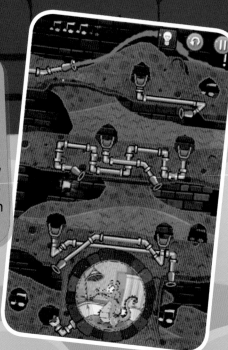

Guest Star

Complete the level with a special guest star! If your original level was a Swampy level, you play the same level as an Allie or a Cranky one.

Duck Swap

The objective of the level stays the same, but the Duckies are switched! So for example, you'll still need to get the water to Swampy, but to tri-duck the level you'll have to collect Cranky's Duckies with poison water.

Where's my collectible?

It doesn't matter what the location is, strange objects can still be found in the dirt. Check which levels they're hidden in below so you can proudly display them on the canal side.

The Sewers

Gnorbet,
Level 4 'Floodgate'

Hank the Tyre Pile,
Level 14 'Just Add Water'

Bingo the Flamingo,
Level 8 'Steam Conductor'

The Soap Factory

Duckie de Milo, Level 22
'Purple Mountains Majesty'

McSoapy Brand Soap,
Level 18 'U-Turn'

Chair-so-soft, Level 26
'Rise and Fall of the Green Empire'

The Beach

Crabby's House,
Level 40 'Beach Bum'

Purple Chip,
Level 44 'Out to Launch'

Glass-a-ma-phone,
Level 49 'Meltdown'

The Bayou

Pink Truffle,
Level 65 'Swampboat'

Feather Hat,
Level 59 'Full Circle'

Bang Flip,
Level 71 'Air Force Water'

Winter Woods

Ice Feast,
Level 81 'I See Purple'

Snow Tennis,
Level 92 'Look Before You Leap'

The Feeling of Speed,
Level 87 'Paving the Way'

Power-ups

If you've ever been stuck on a level for a while or are struggling to reach that last little Ducky, don't worry — the power-ups can offer you a helping hand.

You earn power-ups as you progress through the game, but you can buy them in the store, if you want to use more.

Vacuum

With this power-up, the Duckies in the game will suck in any liquids that are near them. To make this power-up extra-awesome, it will only suck up liquids that will fill it. Phew! A very handy power-up if you're struggling to get a Ducky who is slightly off line.

Dropper

With this power-up, the Duckies start almost full so you only need one more drop to get each one of them. It's a Ducky bonus!

Absorber

No matter whose level you're playing or which Duckies you need to get, use this power-up and the Duckies will accept any liquids.

Hints

If you've tried, tried and tried again but you're still struggling with a level, you can click on 'Hint', the light-bulb button in the top right of the screen. This handy guide will take you through the level cut by cut.

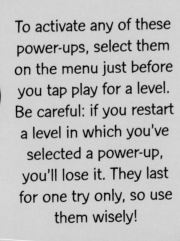

To activate any of these power-ups, select them on the menu just before you tap play for a level. Be careful: if you restart a level in which you've selected a power-up, you'll lose it. They last for one try only, so use them wisely!

Map

SWAMPY

Level 3: Split Second Decision

Get water to Swampy!

Choose a power-up!

Vacuum
Ducks pull their fluids to them!

Dropper
Ducks start almost filled!

Absorber
Ducks accept all fluids!

He's got so many looks!

Rubber Ducky just loves to dress up; he's got so many looks! In WMW2 you can unlock new Ducky costumes.

By now, you'll already have quacked with joy when you noticed that in WMW2, you get your own Rubber Ducky friend to mark your progress through the game. Well, it's about to get even better! If you go to the menu in the bottom left of the home screen and click on the Ducky button, you'll discover that there are lots of new Ducky costumes that can be unlocked! To unlock them, you have to reach certain achievements:

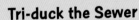

Tri-duck the Sewer

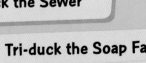

Tri-duck the Soap Factory

Tri-duck the Beach

Send energy to ten friends

Tap on ten friends on the map

Mystery Duck Challenges!

Each time you collect three Mystery Ducks, you can win:

Dino Duck

Unicorn Duck

Gladiator Duck

Marathon Duck

Hula Duck

Space Duck

Keep an eye out for limited edition Duckies which pop up from time to time. You collect these by catching Mystery Duck three times too.

Turn to page 126 to learn more about Mystery Duck.

Did you know?

Swampy's favourite Ducky is Ducky — the original and best.

MYSTERY DUCK

The most magical and mysterious of all the Duckies. No one knows where he might pop up next. All that is known is that once a day, there's a chance to catch him on a level . . . So keep a sharp eye out!

126

When you do find Mystery Duck, there are three types of Mystery Duck levels:

Mystery Duck levels. The level begins and the Mystery Duck appears, but there's no time for amazement because as soon as he appears he moves about the screen, cutting dirt and rock in his wake. You have to catch him on the move! He still needs five drops of water to fill him up.

Duckling levels. On these levels, Mystery Duck transforms himself into ten little ducklings. You have to collect all of them to catch Mystery Duck. Each one of the Ducklings only needs one drop to fill up.

MEGA Duck Levels. On these levels, Mystery Duck transforms himself into the GIANT Mega Duck. To catch Mystery Duck you need to fill this Duck up with 20 drops.

As well as catching Mystery Duck, you'll also need to complete the level, otherwise it won't count.

Good luck!

On Allie
d Cranky levels,
stery Duck turns
o Allie's Mystery
k — catch her with
am — and Cranky's
Mystery Duck —
catch him with
poison water.

Muddy waters

Mud doesn't have to put you into a mud-dle and ruin your perfect game. Here's how it works.

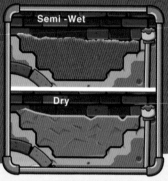

Mud is a semi-dry fluid, which means it will flow but it is thicker and slower than water. If left for long enough it will harden into dirt that you can cut through as normal.

Adding water to mud will keep it wet. How dry the mud is can be gauged by its colour — the more red it is, the wetter it is.

Mud valves shoot out dry mud which will harden on impact.

The mud converter will always shoot out wet mud.

Change it up

Change one fluid into another without the need for Mystery Duck's magic wand!

Converter switches are attached to pipes and will convert any liquid to whichever liquid is shown on the icon.

If there is a lever attached to the converter, you can change the fluid to which the converter will convert.

Why go one way, when you can go another? If you tap these, you can divert the water down a different pipe.

Such a big fan!

Fans blow a column of air that will move fluids
(including steam) in the direction the fan is blowing.

Fans can be activated and
deactivated by switches.

The strength, reach and direction
of each fan is shown by the air
movement above them.

The fans will move all
fluids and steam.

Fans can be attached
to rails so they
can be moved.

Up it goes!

Vacuums are attached to pipes and will suck up any fluids.

Vacuums can be activated and deactivated by switches.

Vacuums can be attached to rails so they can be moved.

Vacuums can pick up balloons.

Meet Swampy!

Down in the sewer there are lots of alligators who just love playing in the mud and chewing on anything they can find . . . mainly pipes. But there's one little gator, Swampy, who loves nothing more than a refreshing and clean shower. Can you spot him climbing into his shower? Yes? Hmm, it might be time for Swampy to start closing his blinds.

Sink or Swim?

Swampy's bathtub is always half full, so no matter what he finds he can always turn it into a treasure — even here at the city dump. While most of the other gators are hunting for some delicious garbage to eat, Swampy has found a pretty purple bow. Who will he give it to?

Boiling Point

There's nothing quite like a Winter Wonder Wasteland. Allie is enjoying a ride in Swampy's latest contraption and Cranky . . . well, he's trying a Swampy-style approach to getting Allie back by his side. Just do not ask how long it took to get Pushy into that wig, dress and make-up. He looks sew-per though, doesn't he?

Hunger Pains

When Swampy found out it was Cranky's birthday, he insisted that all the gators threw him a surprise birthday party. Unfortunately, it was a bad combination of Cranky's least favourite things — singing, goofy hats and, most importantly, surprises.

Bulking Up!

Swampy was eager to show the gators the moves he had learnt from some old aerobics tapes he found in the dump, so he's taken them all to the old abandoned train yard for a pre-dawn workout. Even Cranky is having fun doing what he does best — holding up the rest of the gators with just one arm.

Magic Show

When Swampy found a chest full of magic tricks, he couldn't wait to put on a show. With his trusty assistant, Allie, and the mysterious Mystery Duck making an appearance, it's sure to be a spellbinding show. Cranky is performing his own magic tricks too, by making things disappear . . . into his stomach.

Scan this code on your
smart phone to download
Where's My Water? goodies!

Alternatively, visit
www.**randomhousechildrens**.co.uk/swampysewers

WHERE'S MY WATER: SWAMPY'S OFFICIAL HANDBOOK
A BANTAM BOOK 978 0 857 51333 5

First published in Great Britain by Bantam,
an imprint of Random House Children's Publishers UK
A Random House Group Company

This edition published 2014

1 3 5 7 9 10 8 6 4 2

The Random House Group Limited supports the Forest Stewardship Council® (FSC®), the leading international forest-certification
organisation. Our books carrying the FSC label are printed on FSC®-certified paper. FSC is the only forest-certificationscheme
supported by the leading environmental organisations, including Greenpeace. Our paper procurement policy can be
found at www.randomhouse.co.uk/environment.

MIX
Paper from
responsible sources
FSC
www.fsc.org
FSC® C020056

Bantam Books are published by Random House Children's Publishers UK,
61–63 Uxbridge Road, London W5 5SA

www.**randomhousechildrens**.co.uk

Addresses for companies within The Random House Group Limited can be found at: www.randomhouse.co.uk/offices.htm
THE RANDOM HOUSE GROUP Limited Reg. No. 954009
A CIP catalogue record for this book is available from the British Library.
Printed in China